LIVING IN
DIFFERENT
ENVIRONMENTS

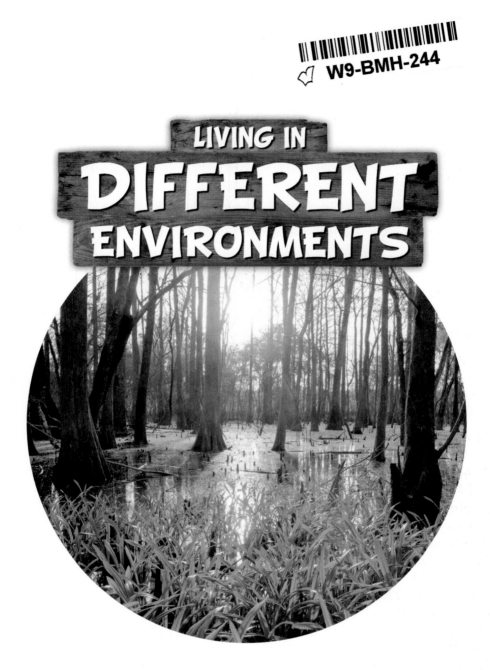

Yanina Ibarra

Literacy Consultants
David Booth • Kathleen Corrigan

Contents

Environments in the United States

The United States is a very big country. It stretches from the Pacific Ocean to the Atlantic Ocean. It has cold states, such as Alaska, and warm states, such as Arizona.

Because the country is so large, it contains many different **environments**. There are dry areas called deserts and wet areas called wetlands. There are mountains and valleys, and large flat areas called plains.

The environments of the United States are not always easy for people to live in. However, people can make changes to the land. These changes allow people to make a home where it may have been hard to live before.

Long ago, only **indigenous** peoples lived in North America. They took from the land only what they needed to **survive**. By the early 1500s, people from Europe had arrived. They used the land and changed it in different ways.

People are always finding new ways to live in the environment around them. Sometimes they make changes to the land itself, but they also change themselves.

Living in the Desert

Deserts cover a huge area in the western United States. They stretch from Oregon and Idaho in the north to Mexico in the south.

A desert is a place that doesn't get much rain. Most deserts in the United States are dry and hot. There are strong winds that can cause dust storms.

Great Basin Desert

Mojave Desert

Chihuahuan Desert

Sonoran Desert

Deserts are very hard places to live in. Many kinds of plants and animals can survive in the desert, but it is difficult for humans. The **lack** of rain is a big problem. But over time, people have found ways to solve this problem.

Did You Know?

Some people who work outdoors in the desert start very early in the morning. This way, they work in the cooler hours. It gets hotter later in the day.

Indigenous groups, such as the Navajo, have lived in deserts for thousands of years. The Navajo came up with ways to be able to farm in deserts, even though there is not much rain. They used **irrigation** to grow crops. For example, they collected water from a stream or a river and used it to water their crops.

People from Spain arrived in the Chihuahuan Desert in the 1500s. They brought new tools for farming. These tools changed the way people lived in the desert.

The Navajo people build homes called hogans. Hogans were traditionally built with materials found in the desert, such as wood and mud.

Irrigation is still used in the desert. For example, farmers can use sprinkler systems to water large areas of crops at one time.

There is not much water in the desert, but there are other natural **resources** people can use. Deserts are a good source of **solar** and wind energy. Solar power plants in the deserts turn sunlight into electricity. Wind **turbine** farms use wind to create electricity. Having electricity makes life in the desert much more comfortable.

When wind blows, it makes the blades of a wind turbine spin. The blades are connected to a generator. The spinning motion powers the generator and makes electricity.

Living in the Appalachian Mountains

The Appalachian Mountains run along the East Coast of North America from Canada to Alabama. The Appalachians can be more than 6,000 feet high in some areas. High in the mountains, there are usually very strong winds and cold temperatures. The air is warmer near the bottom of the mountains.

The Appalachian Mountains have many different plants, animals, and minerals. There are also many springs, streams, waterfalls, and rivers. Heavy rains and snowstorms may cause floods.

Appalachian Mountains

Many indigenous groups have lived in the Appalachian Mountains, including the Pennacook in the north and the Cherokee in the south. They hunted, fished, and farmed in the mountains and valleys.

The Appalachian Mountains are covered by forests. Plants and fruits from the Appalachian forests were important in indigenous peoples' diets. However, not all plants were safe to eat. Other useful resources in the mountains included wood, iron, and stone.

This is what the Algonquian village of Pomeiooc looked like in 1585. The huts and longhouses were surrounded by a fence. The fence protected the village from enemies.

This is an old house from the 1800s. It is located in the Great Smoky Mountains near Gatlinburg, Tennessee.

In the 1700s, many people from Europe came to live in the Appalachian Mountains. They first settled in the central area of the mountains. They reached Pennsylvania, Virginia, and Tennessee. The settlers used resources from the forest to build communities.

In the late 1800s, there were many factories and railroads in the United States. These factories and railroads needed fuel to run. They used coal as fuel. There is a lot of coal in the Appalachian Mountains, so many people who lived there started working as coal miners.

The earliest coal mines were dirty and dangerous. Over time, many miners moved to cities or looked for other kinds of jobs. Today coal is still mined in the Appalachian Mountains. Coal mining is much less dangerous, thanks to modern machines.

This photograph from 1908 shows workers in a West Virginia coal mine.

Fort William Henry in Lake George, New York, is a museum and a popular tourist attraction.

Now people visit the Appalachian Mountains area to enjoy its natural resources. Tourism and recreation are growing industries. These can be **sustainable** businesses. They can create new jobs without harming natural resources. The Appalachian National Scenic Trail is one example. It is a path that stretches across 14 states. Many people come from all over to hike along the trail. There are a lot of trail-related jobs as well, such as guides and maintenance workers.

Living in the Wetlands

Wetlands connect water and land. Examples of wetlands are swamps, marshes, and bogs. There are two types of wetlands in the United States: tidal wetlands and nontidal wetlands. Tidal wetlands lie along the coast and reach the ocean. Nontidal wetlands make up most of the U.S. wetlands. They can be found all over the country.

Wetlands clean and store water and hold back floods. They are a good place for many plants, animals, and insects to live.

Wetlands

People in the United States did not always think wetlands were important. In the 1700s, settlers thought wetlands made people sick. Settlers also drained many wetlands so that the land could be used for farming.

Did You Know?

More than 110 million acres of wetlands in the United States have been lost since the 1700s.

People's opinions about wetlands changed over time. People started to see them as natural resources. Once people's opinions about wetlands changed, many laws and parks were created to help take care of them. Many trained people are needed to do this work. They need to know about local plants, animals, and the land.

Did You Know?

Mosquitoes and many other insects live in the wetlands.

Living on the Great Plains

The Great Plains stretch from the Arctic Ocean all the way to the Rio Grande. They lie between the Rocky Mountains and the Mississippi River.

These lands have low hills and valleys. The Missouri River, Rio Grande, and Arkansas River help drain the plains. The area is covered with green grass. Summers are very warm, and winters are cold.

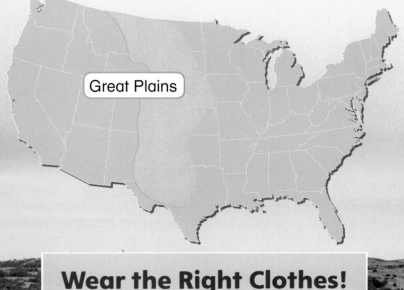

Great Plains

Wear the Right Clothes!

It can get very cold in the winter on the plains. Always dress warmly.

Until the 1500s, only indigenous people lived on the Great Plains. They hunted and traveled on foot. Then people from Spain brought horses to the plains. Horses made it easier to hunt and travel in such a large area. More people started moving to the plains.

In the 1800s, it became even easier to travel across the plains. The train had been invented, and railroads were built. People who had farms could travel to towns and sell what they grew. They could buy what they needed in town and then return to their home in the country.

Watch for Tornadoes!
Spring to early summer is tornado season in the Great Plains **region**.

In the past, trains such as this one had steam engines.

Today there are a few large cities and some towns in the plains. People have invented even better ways of traveling long distances, such as cars and buses. These inventions make it easier to live on the Great Plains.

A lot of wheat is grown in the Great Plains region. In 2016, Kansas State produced almost 500 million bushels of wheat.

Changing the Land

The United States is a huge country. It has many different environments, including deserts, mountains, wetlands, and plains.

Today much of the land looks very different from when only indigenous groups lived here. As more people came to live in the United States, they slowly changed the land.

Although many changes have made life easier, some changes have also had negative effects. Human activity has caused pollution and destroyed much of the natural environment. This destruction affects not only people but plants and animals as well.

Today more people understand the importance of taking care of the land. They are taking steps to protect the different regions of the United States.

Glossary

environments: the conditions in which people, animals, and plants live

indigenous: native to a particular area

irrigation: a particular way of supplying land with water

lack: the state of being without something or not having enough of something

region: area

resources: materials; supplies

solar: from the sun

survive: stay alive

sustainable: relating to methods that try to preserve nature

turbine: a machine for producing power

Index